The Lakota
People, Culture, and History

by Tracy Hauff

CAPSTONE PRESS
a capstone imprint

Published by Capstone Press, an imprint of Capstone
1710 Roe Crest Drive, North Mankato, Minnesota 56003
capstonepub.com

Library of Congress Cataloging-in-Publication Data is available on the Library of Congress website.

ISBN: 9798875208423 (hardcover)
ISBN: 9798875208379 (paperback)
ISBN: 9798875208386 (ebook PDF)

Summary: The traditions, culture, and history of the Lakota people are told through engaging text, sidebars, activities, maps, and more.

Editorial Credits
Editor: Erika L. Shores; Designer: Heidi Thompson; Media Researcher: Rebekah Hubstenberger; Production Specialist: Tori Abraham

Image Credits
Alamy: imageBROKER.com GmbH & Co. KG, 7, Nancy Carter/North Wind Picture Archives, 28, Penta Springs Limited, 26, Richard Tsong-Taatarii/Minneapolis Star Tribune via ZUMA Press Inc, 6, World History Archive, 13; Associated Press: Hannah Hunsinger/Rapid City Journal, 16, Matthew Brown, 19, Rapid City Journal/Chris Huber, 29; Getty Images: Andy Cross/The Denver Post, 17, Archive Photos/Hulton Archive, 10, Bettmann, 11, Dia Dipasupil, 20, Fine Art, 24, Hulton Archive, 14, iStock/CharlotteMB, cover, Jerry Holt/The Minnesota Star Tribune, 22 (bottom), Nikki Kahn/The Washington Post, 21; Paul Szabo, Sicangu Lakota, Rosebud Reservation, original artwork drawn in a ledger book from 1900, photographed by Tracy Hauff, 9; Shutterstock: Iker Zabaleta, 27, MaraZe, 23, Pyty, 5, Runrun2 (brush stroke), back cover, spine, 1; The Metropolitan Museum of Art: The Charles and Valerie Diker Collection of Native American Art, Gift of Charles and Valerie Diker, 2018 & 2019, 18, 22 (top left)

Printed and bound in the USA. 006307

TABLE OF CONTENTS

Words in **bold** are in the glossary.

ABOUT THE LAKOTA

Who Are the Lakota?

The Lakota, Dakota, and Nakota people are divisions of the **Indigenous** group known as the Oceti Sakowin—the Seven Council Fires. These groups are distinguished by differences in dialect. A dialect means that the language varies depending on geographic region. The Lakota Oyate (oh-ya-tay) is the largest division. Traditionally, the Lakota were nomadic, following buffalo herds on the Great Plains. This area is now the states of Montana, Wyoming, Colorado, Nebraska, North Dakota, and South Dakota.

What Does *Lakota* Mean?

Lakota means "ally" or "friend." The Lakota people should not be called "Sioux," even though they are referred to as the Great Sioux Nation. The name "Sioux" originated when French traders met with the Ojibwe tribes, who were Lakota enemies. The Ojibwe described the Lakota to the French as Nadowessioux, meaning "little snakes." The French shortened the term to "Sioux," and this name was widely adopted by **colonizers**, who believed it was correct.

Where Do the Lakota Live Today?

Seven Lakota tribes live on six **reservations** in South Dakota, North Dakota, and Montana. The combined population of these six reservations is around 100,000 citizens. The reservations are spread out in rural areas with few job opportunities.

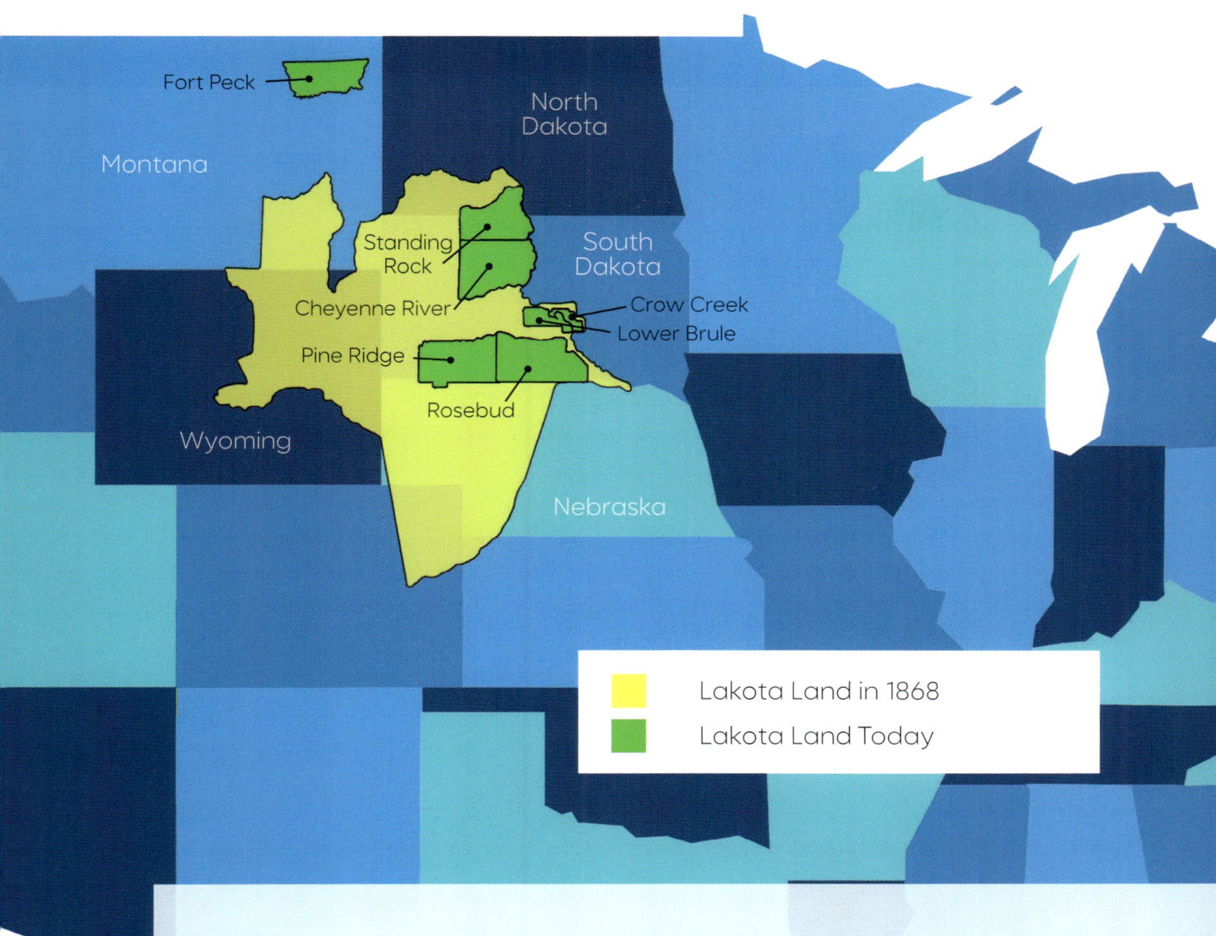

Lakota Tribal Reservations

Hunkpapa	Standing Rock Reservation and Fort Peck Reservation
Itazipcho	Cheyenne River Reservation
Mniconjou	Cheyenne River Reservation
Oglala	Pine Ridge Reservation
Oohenupa	Cheyenne River Reservation
Sicangu	Rosebud Reservation and Lower Brule Reservation
Sihasapa	Cheyenne River Reservation

LAKOTA GATHERINGS

The Lakota word for dance is wacipi (wah-chee-pee). Every summer, Lakota gather for celebrations of music, dancing, and singing called wacipis, or powwows. These gatherings are an exciting time for Lakota families. They reconnect, meet new relatives, and celebrate their traditions.

Families travel in vans, campers, or customized trailers to powwows. The vehicles carry dancing **regalia** and serve as a place to sleep. Some people sleep in tipis to honor their **culture**. Regalia is the colorful clothing that powwow dancers wear. Relatives help sew the dresses, shirts, and pants. Beads, porcupine quills, and feathers are added to the clothing.

Each Lakota reservation hosts an outdoor powwow on different weekends from June through August.

A dancer takes part in the Oglala Lakota Nation Powwow in South Dakota.

The Lakota have always been admired for their artistic abilities, and use their skills as artists and dancers to make a living. The powwow is an event where they display these talents. Artists set up booths surrounding the powwow arena to sell beadwork, quillwork, leatherwork, and paintings. Dancers, accompanied by drum groups and singers, compete for prizes. The drum, known as "the heartbeat of the people," is an essential part of the powwow.

LAKOTA HISTORY

More than 400 years ago, Lakota ancestors lived near the Great Lakes in what is today Minnesota and Wisconsin. Conflicts with other Indigenous groups forced them to move farther west to the Great Plains. In the 1700s, the Lakota began using horses to hunt. They became skilled hunters who moved from place to place, following the buffalo herds.

The Lakota peoples' first significant encounter with Euro-Americans happened in 1804. U.S. President Thomas Jefferson sent Meriwether Lewis and William Clark to explore territory gained in the Louisiana Purchase. The journey took them north on the Missouri River, deep into Lakota lands.

Lewis and Clark reported back to President Jefferson about the plentiful wild game, large herds of buffalo, and beautiful prairies. Jefferson was eager to pursue his vision of Westward Expansion, adding land west of the Mississippi River to the United States. He didn't consider that some of this land was already home to Lakota tribes, people who had no intention of giving up their cherished homeland.

Paul Szabo, Pehan Manni (Walking Crane), Sicangu Lakota artist from the Rosebud Reservation created "Adrift." The drawing portrays the keelboat of Lewis and Clark on the Missouri River in 1804 when they first met the Lakota people. It was drawn in colored pencil on ledger paper from 1900.

After the expedition, increasing numbers of Euro-Americans arrived on the Great Plains. The Lakota liked the settlers' tools and supplies. The two groups traded with each other at fur trading posts. Lakota were willing to be friends with the settlers. However, the U.S. government had already decided they wanted the territory for themselves and sent soldiers to remove the Lakota.

Red Cloud, an important Oglala Lakota leader, led Red Cloud's War in the Powder River area in Wyoming and Montana territories. Between 1866 and 1868, he and his warriors destroyed newly built railroad tracks and burned down military forts along the Bozeman Trail. Crazy Horse was another powerful Oglala Lakota warrior the U.S. Cavalry feared. He fought alongside Red Cloud.

Chief Red Cloud

Red Cloud was born in 1821 and rose to power in 1841. He led Red Cloud's War to stop the U.S. government from building forts along the Bozeman Trail. Before starting the war, he made this speech to his people: "Hear me, Lakota. Yet before the ashes of the council fire are cold, the Great Father (the U.S. president) is building forts among us. His presence here is an insult and a threat. It is an insult to the spirits of our ancestors. Are we to give up their sacred grounds to be plowed for corn? Lakota, I am for war." He was a courageous warrior and an intelligent speaker. The U.S. government respected his leadership qualities.

The signing of the Treaty of Fort Laramie ended Red Cloud's War in 1868.

The U.S. government wrote the **Treaty** of Fort Laramie in 1868 to end Red Cloud's War. The treaty gave the Lakota the land they wanted, including the sacred Black Hills. Satisfied, the Lakota stopped making war, and returned to the lands where they hunted.

The United States broke the Treaty of Fort Laramie in 1874. The government sent U.S. General George Armstrong Custer on a gold-seeking expedition into the Black Hills. Gold was discovered. The Black Hills filled with people who were determined to dig up the sacred ground of the Lakota in search of gold.

In the summer of 1876, 8,000 Lakota, Cheyenne, and Arapaho people were camped in Montana. They had gathered for a buffalo hunt and annual Sun Dance. The camps of people stretched several miles long.

The U.S. 7th Cavalry learned of their location and planned a surprise attack. They did not know the camp included 2,000 of the Lakota's bravest warriors. These warriors were led by Crazy Horse, Sitting Bull, Chief Hump, and Chief Gall. Custer's scouts warned him that he was outnumbered. But he did not listen. The warriors overpowered the 7th Cavalry, and not one soldier from Custer's regiment survived.

A painting from around 1900 by Amos Bad Heart Buffalo shows warriors leading away horses captured after the battle with Custer.

After the United States lost the battle, known as the Battle of the Little Bighorn, the Lakota faced terrible consequences. The U.S. government ordered the Lakota to surrender to reservations. The Lakota were pursued. Many innocent Lakota men, women, and children were killed.

The government tried to force the Lakota to give up their traditional lifestyle by taking their children and placing them in **boarding schools**. The Carlisle Indian Industrial School in Pennsylvania was opened. Children from Lakota families involved in the Battle of the Little Bighorn were among the first students. The children weren't allowed to wear their traditional clothing at the school. Their braids were cut off. They were punished for speaking the Lakota language. The government wanted to erase their culture completely.

In 1890, two weeks after the killing of Sitting Bull, the 7th Cavalry killed 300 unarmed Lakota at Wounded Knee Creek on the Pine Ridge Reservation. The massacre destroyed the Lakota peoples' hope of ever returning to a nomadic life on the Great Plains.

Sitting Bull

Sitting Bull, a Hunkpapa Lakota spiritual leader and powerful war chief, was born around 1834. He refused to surrender after the battle with Custer, escaping with his band to live in Canada. In 1881, he returned to the United States, saying, "My people are cold and hungry. My women are sick and my children freezing. I will do as the Great Father (the U.S. president) wishes. I will give my guns and ponies into his hands. My arrows are broken and my war paint thrown to the wind." He surrendered and settled on the Standing Rock Reservation. James McLaughlin, the reservation's Indian agent, ordered his arrest. Sitting Bull resisted and was killed in his home in December 1890. He was a hero to the Lakota people.

Timeline

1804	The first Euro-American contact with the Lakota
1849	Fort Laramie is established as the principal military post and trading center in Lakota country.
1866-1868	Red Cloud's War
1868	The Treaty of Fort Laramie is signed by the Lakota and Arapaho people.
1874	Gold is discovered in the Black Hills by the Custer Expedition.
1876	Battle of the Little Bighorn
1877	Crazy Horse is killed at Fort Robinson.
1879	The Carlisle Indian Industrial School opens in Pennsylvania.
1890	Sitting Bull is killed in his home at Standing Rock Reservation.
1890	The Wounded Knee Massacre of 300 Lakota
1924	The Indian Citizenship Act is signed by President Calvin Coolidge, giving Indians the right to vote.
1964	Billy Mills, Oglala Lakota, wins a gold medal in the Olympics.
1980	The U.S. Supreme Court rules that the Black Hills legally belong to the Lakota.
2004	Cecilia Fire Thunder is elected the first female president of the Oglala Lakota tribe.
2012	The Rosebud and Standing Rock Tribes purchase Pe'Sla, a sacred Lakota site.
2015	Shannon County, containing the Pine Ridge Reservation, is renamed the Oglala Lakota County.
2016 –2017	Water protectors along with several Indigenous groups at Standing Rock protest and stop the construction of an oil pipeline through reservation lands.
2021	The Oglala Lakota Artspace, the first community art facility in Pine Ridge, is opened in Kyle, South Dakota.
2024	The remains of three children who died at the Carlisle boarding school are returned to Pine Ridge.

LAKOTA CULTURE

Mitakuye oyasin (me-ta-coo-yay oh-yah-seen) means everyone is related and must treat one another as they would like to be treated. The Lakota apply this to humans, animals, plants, water, and Mother Earth. If a person takes something from Mother Earth, such as eating a plant, they must thank her for the gift. The person returns the favor by properly caring for the soil, water, and seeds that go into growing the plant.

Students on the Pine Ridge Reservation pause after a nature hike near their school.

The Seven Lakota Values

Mitakuye oyasin goes hand-in-hand with wolakota. This is the behavior that sustains peace and friendship. This code of behavior is based on the seven Lakota values:

Compassion: Take care of those who are suffering.

Generosity: Help others by sharing what you have.

Honesty: Do not take what does not belong to you. Be truthful in your words.

Humility: Do not be arrogant and expect rewards for good deeds.

Prayer: Pray to the Creator for yourself and others, be thankful.

Respect: Treat all living beings on Earth with dignity and kindness.

Wisdom: Open your eyes, ears, and mind to learning; wisdom is a gift.

A Lakota child offers sage smoke. This tradition is said to bring healing, positivity, and balance.

THE BUFFALO NATION

The buffalo has long been at the center of Lakota life. Traditionally, buffalo provided food, shelter, clothing, utensils, tools, and weapons. Lakota called themselves P'te Oyate (puh–tay oh-ya-tay), the Buffalo Nation. Lakota men hunted and provided protection to their nation. Lakota women were necessary to the nation's survival too. They easily took apart the tipis, which was necessary for quickly moving camp when buffalo herds approached.

A cover for a Lakota tipi from 1890 has Lakota warriors on horseback painted on it.

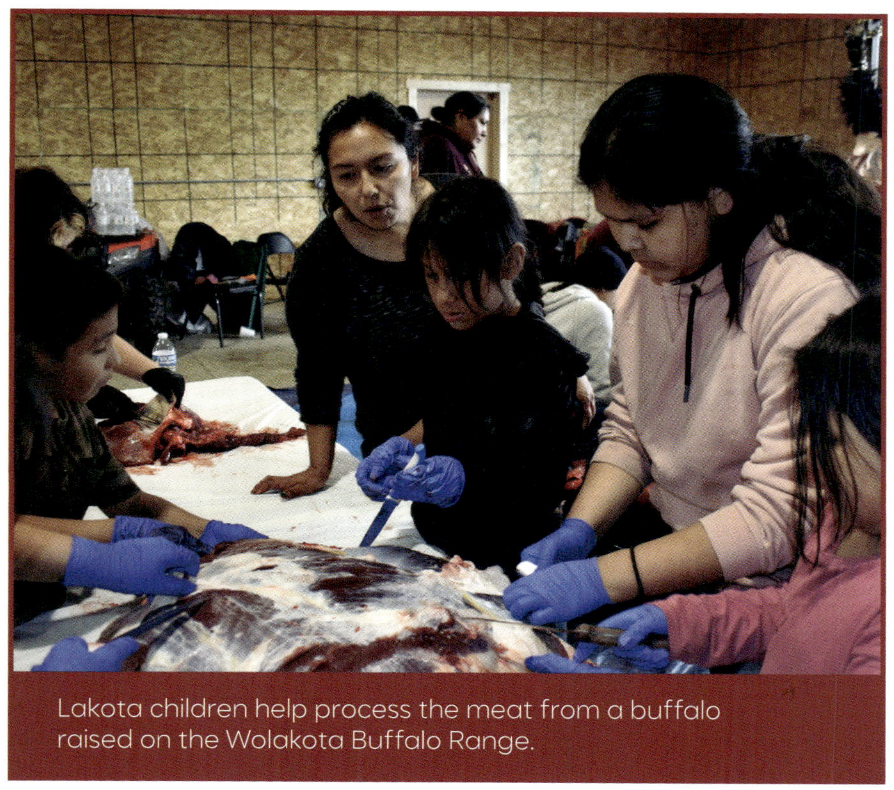

Lakota children help process the meat from a buffalo raised on the Wolakota Buffalo Range.

The U.S. government knew if they destroyed the Lakota's source of food and shelter, the people would become weak and defenseless. They encouraged buffalo hunters to kill the buffalo and take their hides. The hunters left behind the rotting bodies of the animals across the plains. The buffalo was almost completely wiped out. In recent years, buffalo numbers have increased due to the efforts of tribal organizations. Lakota tribes now manage and harvest buffalo from their own herds. The butchering of the buffalo is performed in a joyful traditional ceremony.

In Lakota tradition, boys began learning survival skills as young as four. This started with their first bow and arrows. They learned to ride bareback on colts and became accomplished riders by their teens. Boys played hunting and war games to build strength, swiftness, and endurance.

Horses still play an important role in Lakota culture. Children learn to ride at a young age. Many young riders participate in races and rodeos. Lakota children used to ride horses to school. Some still use horses to travel short distances today.

Larissa FastHorse

Larissa FastHorse, Sicangu Lakota, is a playwright with many firsts. In 2000, she attended the United Nations Conference as a delegate representing Native film writers and producers. She is the first American Indian female to have a play produced on Broadway. She recently revised the Peter Pan theater script to remove prejudiced scenes. FastHorse said, "My goal in this was that every child that comes to this show will leave the theatre and believe they can look out their window and see Peter fly by. Not a Victorian child's window, not a wealthy child's window, not a white child's window. They can believe *their* window, that Peter will come to them."

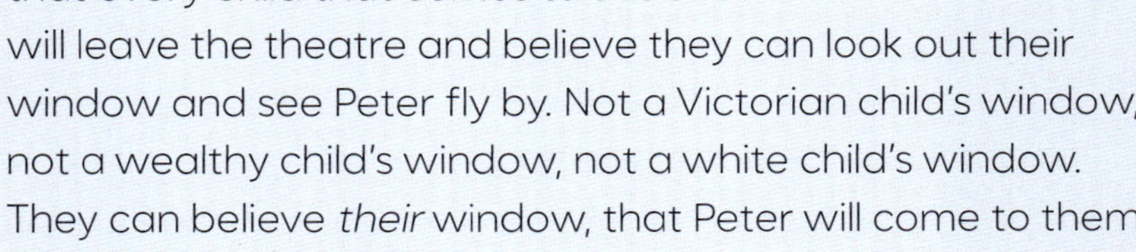

Many Lakota children grow up riding horses.

A Lakota dress from 1870

Lakota girls were taught sewing, quilling, and beading. Before fur traders introduced glass beads, porcupine quills were the main material used for decoration. Women took great pride in adorning their family's buckskin clothing, moccasins, and leather bags. Lakota beading is identified by geometric patterns and is used for ornamentation today.

A Lakota artist works on a beading project.

A Lakota Recipe

The Lakota ate wasna while traveling and during the cold winter months. In the old days, the Lakota would grind the ingredients using a pounding stone. For this recipe, ask an adult to help you use a food processor.

Ingredients

- 2 cups cooked shredded beef or bison jerky
- 1 cup chopped tart berries, such as chokecherries, buffalo berries, or cranberries
- 6 tablespoons beef tallow or vegetable shortening

Instructions

1. Using a food processor, shred the jerky and berries.
2. Melt the tallow or shortening. Stir it into the beef mixture until mixed well.
3. Form the mixture into flat patties.
4. Eat and enjoy!

Keep wasna in the fridge and eat within three days. If you want to store them, you can dry the patties in a food dehydrator.

THE WINTER COUNT

An important part of Lakota tradition is keeping a record of past years. This record is known as the winter count. Traditionally, one major event was painted on a buffalo hide to document each year. A respected male tribal member was responsible for this task until he left for the spirit world. The responsibility was then passed to a younger male relative.

The winter count keeper met with tribal members to decide which event from the year should be recorded. As the buffalo herd decreased, the Lakota continued the winter count on fabrics introduced by the white settlers, such as muslin, linen, or canvas. The winter count began in the center of the hide and moved in a spiral from left to right. Some Lakota tribal communities continue the tradition today.

Make Your Own Winter Count

Study the winter count photo on page 24 to see how the Lakota used drawings to record events. In the center, a human figure is covered in red dots, representing the year that many Lakota people died from the smallpox disease. What might the other drawings mean? Think about your family history and create your own winter count.

What You Need

- cloth fabric, brown craft paper, or construction paper
- scissors
- fabric markers, paint, colored pencils, or crayons

What You Do

1. Draw a buffalo hide shape on fabric or paper and cut it out.
2. You can start in the center with the year you were born. You can draw a picture of you as a baby.
3. Think of other important events in your family or community. Draw pictures for the years your brothers or sisters were born. You can draw your school for the year you started. Draw when you got your pets or a special holiday. Draw whatever has made each year memorable for you and your family.

THE SUN DANCE

The Sun Dance is the most sacred ceremony for the Lakota. It is performed each summer. The U.S. government outlawed the Sun Dance in 1883. But the Lakota continued to practice it secretly, risking being put in jail. Performing the Sun Dance today is legal.

Men pierce their chests with skewers of sharpened sticks or bones. Leather strips are attached to the skewers and to a section of a cottonwood tree. The dancers go without eating or drinking for days. They pray to the Creator while pulling away from the tree.

A painting from 1895 shows people taking part in the Sun Dance ceremony.

A fire burns outside the sweat lodge where the inipi ceremony takes place.

Another important Lakota ritual is the inipi (ee-knee-pee). Sundancers must participate in this purification ceremony. The inipi takes place in a sweat lodge. The lodge is made from red willow branches shaped into a dome and covered with animal hides or canvas. Inside, it is dark with a dirt floor. Outside, a firekeeper tends the fire to keep the stones hot. They are carried inside with deer antlers, and hot water is poured over the rocks to create steam.

A tree used in the Sun Dance ceremony

The Sun Dance is done as an offering to ensure the well-being of the Lakota community. Families camp by their Sun Dance tree for a week during this ceremony. Out of respect, no photographs are allowed of the ritual. Once the ceremony is over and the families have gone home, the tree stands alone on the prairie, a beautiful symbol of hope and renewal.

Lakota artwork, horse-riding expertise, the Sun Dance, and inipi are core traditions passed down to each generation. At the heart of the Lakota culture is their language. Once forbidden by the U.S. government, it is now taught in reservation schools. The first Lakota language book written by a Lakota teacher, Albert White Hat, was published in 1999. Lakota language classes now begin in kindergarten. Preserving their language protects the unique culture that defines the Lakota people.

The Lakota Language

The Lakota work to keep their language alive. They want to remember it and teach it to their children. Here are some words to learn in Lakota.

anpetu was'te (ahn-pay-to wash-day)—good day

até (ah-tay)—father

hanhepi was'te (hah-heh-pee wash-day)—good night

iná (ee-nah)—mother

lala (la-la)—grandpa

toksa aké (doke-sha ah-kay)—see you later

unci (oon-chee)—grandma

wacipi (wah-chee-pee)—dance

wopila (whoa-pee-la)—thank you

Glossary

boarding school (BOR-ding SKOOL)—a place where students live while they are going to school at the same time

colonizer (KAH-luh-nye-zur)—a nation or government that claims a territory other than its own

culture (KUHL-chur)—the traditions, beliefs, and behaviors that a group of people share

Indigenous (in-DIJ-eh-nus)—the first to live in a place

regalia (re-GALE-ee-uh)—special clothes that are worn for powwows or other special occasions

reservation (rez-er-VAY-shuhn)—an area of land that has been set aside for a tribe or tribes under an agreement with the U.S. government

treaty (TREE-tee)—a written agreement between two groups

Read More

Phillips, Katrina M. *Powwows*. North Mankato, MN: Capstone, 2026.

Sorell, Traci. *We Are Still Here!: Native American Truths Everyone Should Know*. Watertown, MA: Charlesbridge, 2021.

Treuer, Anton. *Everything You Wanted to Know About Indians But Were Afraid to Ask*. Hoboken, NJ: Levine Querido, 2021.

Internet Sites

Lakota Culture: Beliefs and Traditions
aktalakota.stjo.org/lakota-culture/beliefs-traditions

Oglala Sioux Tribe: The Pine Ridge Indian Reservation
oglala.gov

Rosebud Sioux Tribe: History and Culture
rosebudsiouxtribe-nsn.gov/history-culture

Index

About the Author

Tracy Hauff is an enrolled member of the Oglala Lakota Oyate from the Pine Ridge Reservation in South Dakota. She is the author of *Blending Cultures: A Journey of Identity in Lakota Country* and *Far From the Forest*. Her influential essays, short stories, and poetry have been published by the University of Nebraska Press, University of Minnesota Press, CAIRNS Press, Wíčazo Ša Review, and Studies in American Indian Literature. She is a member of the Oceti Sakowin Writers Society, contributing to the rich tapestry of Indigenous literature.